Bullshit,

non-sense

and

common-sense

about

meditation

A semi-serious introduction and a
sequence of thoughts and
experiences

By Dr Mariette Jansen (Dr De-Stress)

Published in 2013

ISBN number 9781849144551

Copyright @2013 by Dr Mariette Jansen

How to contact Dr Mariette Jansen

Email: mariette@stressfreecoaching.co.uk

LinkedIn: http://www.linkedin.com/pub/dr-mariette-jansen-dr-de-stress/28/a13/839

Website: http://www.stressfreecoaching.co.uk

Facebook: www.facebook.com/DrDeStress

Twitter @Mariette_Jansen

Prologue

Yes, I did it! I wrote down my thoughts, went through the motions of tedious editing and formatting, re-writing, and skipping and at last published. My first! It feels like giving birth and it has a similar sense of relief and happiness, once the baby is disconnected from its source and healthily breathing on its own.

Thanks to all those supportive people around me, who facilitated me and gave me the time and energy to go through the process and especially the honesty from Christine, Kathy, Beth, Ann, Zoe, Karen, Miriam and Jill, in their straight feedback. A special thanks to my 'tante Wil', who designed the cover. And all those who had to listen to my obsessive chats about it.

I hope you get a sparkle of my thoughts and ideas on how you can use magical meditation to improve your life, but just get started by enjoying this book.

Go well,

Mariette

Table of content

8

Introduction

I jotted down the 'work title' for this book as 'Bullshit and (non)sense about meditation', changed it slightly in the end. But, why did I want to write a book about a subject so close to my heart with such a 'jokey' title? Don't I take it seriously? Am I just taking the mickey?

I am extremely serious and passionate about the concept, the techniques and the skill of meditation. I am also extremely annoyed with the veil of mystery, new-ageism, and almost cult scene approach that surrounds the topic. Breathing in love and peace, spending hours a day practicing, being highly spiritual and going for enlightenment…..This non-sense creates a barrier for a lot of people, who would benefit from meditation but are put off or uncomfortable by the bull shit.

Mediation is natural to humans. Babies retreat when they don't want to take in any more information, and if we hadn't lost touch with our natural state of being, we all would retreat at regular times. However, busy life styles don't allow time to respond to that need and we have gradually de-learned how to de-stress with meditation techniques.

The fact we have de-learned, means we can re-learn and as it is an essential part of being human, easy to do and getting quick results.
Meditation is for everyone, it supports general health, well-being and happiness and should be part of everybody's set of life skills. It is available: regardless of gender, age, cultural background, religion, physical health, and it doesn't require any tools or equipment.

Meditation practice is also accessible from everywhere; as just a 1 minute practice will do, you can do it while waiting for the traffic lights, standing in a queue or coming back from the toilet.
What better stress management tool than meditation? Natural, easy and available, always and everywhere!

I believe that the world would be a better place if everybody meditated, so my mission is to get everybody practicing. As meditation is simple, down-to-earth, easy, and fun, there is no excuse not to practice it.

This booklet is offering easy accessible information on the topic, some anecdotes about my own experience and food for thought, in the hope it encourages you, my reader, to start experimenting and finding out how meditation practice can improve your life.

When I read about research and studies, I always try to 'translate' the information into a framework and language that make sense to me. It simplifies complex studies and even though, it might not always cover all aspects of the research, I make it work for me. In sharing it with you, I hope to make it work for you. Don't hang me up on the total accuracy, just take from it what you like and what resonates with you.

I have been using meditation in my work as a therapist, counsellor and life coach, and have been teaching it for the last 10 years: in schools, privately and in fitness centres. I have seen how non-meditators easily pick up the techniques and I have received very positive feedback. If it works for all those others, why would it not work for you?

Go well, and enjoy!

Mariette

Chapter 1 Bullshit, non-sense and common-sense

Welcome to what is meant to be a refreshing, light, amusing and SERIOUS book about a topic close to my heart and a necessity for my happiness: MINDFULNESS MEDITATION.

I have always been drawn to meditation, that intriguing activity or non-activity. When I was younger, I actually did not know what it was, but still loved the idea. Occasionally, I did short courses, always enjoyable, but never offering me the clarity and guidance I was looking for. I practiced in my own way, with guided tapes, guidelines from self-help books and what I took away from different weekends and training sessions.
I liked what I did. But as it did not have any structure, I struggled with the discipline.

The change
As a busy working mum, time is precious and needs to be approached with TLC. I can be pretty efficient, but got myself in a bit of panic when a few years ago I was asked to do a course: 1.5 days a week for 6 weeks. That in itself doesn't sound too demanding, but as my week was carefully and fully planned, I faced the challenge of finding 1.5 days ...

I made a decision that may sound counterproductive: I got up 45 minutes earlier than I needed to and did a meditation. I was already meditating regularly, putting it into my planning for the day. But as happened, when 'life got in the way' I had to give my meditation a miss. Not so when it was rigidly scheduled as the first action of the day. I was truly amazed by the benefits: I felt physically fitter, more focussed, calmer and got through those 6 weeks with no issues.

And I have never looked back since. Every morning, at 6am the latest, I will be 'sitting' for half an hour.

If I get a bit easy on the habit, I pay a price: I am less efficient, easier hit by moods and emotions, nervous and feeling overwhelmed.

Why is it, that meditation gives me more benefits than sleep?

When we sleep, we try to rest our body. But do we? How much tension are we holding onto in our sleep? How many people are clenching their fists, grinding their teeth and tensing their shoulders during the nightly hours?

Conclusion: sleep doesn't ensure we rest our body.

When we sleep, we try to rest our mind. But do we? How many problems do we solve tossing and turning?

How many adventures and challenges can we face during our dreams?

Conclusion: sleep doesn't ensure we rest our mind.

Meditation however, does rest the body; as you make the conscious effort to relax your body you will notice where you hold tension and you can let go. It is amazing how there is always tension somewhere in your body......
Meditation also gives the mind a rest; as you make the continuous effort to focus and concentrate, the mind has no other choice than to obey. Of course, your mind will wander off, but as you bring it back to your topic of focus, it will not get the chance to wander all over the place. Hence, you give your mind a rest as well.

The power of one minute

Based on my experiences and the benefits I got from my daily practice I started to bring meditation into my professional life. I was teaching counselling students at the time and my classes usually started with a brief relaxation/meditation – to get everyone into the room! It made it easier for my students to focus on the course, instead of fretting about issues outside the class room. It was highly appreciated, at least by some, as a recent phone call proved. This ex-student called me a few years after his course, to let me know that he was still thinking of the meditation practices we did and how he loved it.

I brought meditation techniques into my teaching, but also into my work with clients. During private counselling sessions, it proved a powerful tool as it helped clients to move away from 'the story' and get in touch with their emotions more easily.

Then I set up my own business, offering counselling, coaching, and meditation tutoring via workshops and individual teaching. Feedback showed that my students loved the experience, understood how it could work for them, but missed a framework or structure to give it a space in their daily lives.

This offered me a challenge, that I could not resist.

The challenge: I want to meditate, but I have no time, am not prepared to put a lot of effort in and will need to be getting quick results

My answer: an online meditation training based on Mariette's-one-minute-meditation (MOMM): The Meditation Wave.

I designed an exercise that lasted only one minute, was easy to do and amazed me with the fantastic results. The exercise involved engaging the breath, focussing the mind and engaging the brain in such a way that body, mind and brain got a break from their usual 'busy-ness' with fantastic results.

This course/technique received Janey Lee Grace's Platinum Award for 'best stress management technique'. A 28 day programme that takes no more than 10 minutes a day and feedback showed how people slept better, felt less anxious, could handle confrontations, reduced their IBS symptoms and overall felt happier.

No non-sense and common-sense

MOMM (Mariette's One Minute Meditation) is just an exercise like any other. Spend 1 minute to focus, do that a few times a day, and harvest the results. There is no option for any excuse; as long as you find time to go to the toilet, or as long as you are faced with waiting for a traffic light, or the kettle to boil, you can find a golden minute for your MOMM. Standing, sitting, walking .... you can do it anywhere!
What this proves is that meditation doesn't need to take place on top of a mountain, with your legs uncomfortably folded in the lotus position and having set aside the next one and a half hours of your day.
You don't need to wear floaty clothes, show the peace sign all the time, talk slowly and smile continuously. You can just be the neurotic city professional with a long things-to-do list, nervously eating your nails and feeling that churn in your tummy. However, once you start doing the one minute exercise, stepping from the

stress-zone into the zen-zone, on a regular basis, you will start noticing a positive difference.

Meditation practice can be done anywhere and everywhere. As long as you look for stress relief, tension reduction and generally want to improve your well-being.

Go ahead!

Chapter 2. A simplified version of the world.....

As I told you in the introduction, I am not a scientist and don't have the intention to be one. I am a collector of information to make sense of my world. The way that I can make sense of what happens when we meditate, is based upon quantum physics (as far as I understand it).
Quantum physics is a branch of science that deals with discrete, indivisible units of energy.

There are 5 basic ideas that form the foundation of the theory:

- Energy is not continuous, but comes in small but discrete units, quantums or particles
- The elementary particles behave both like particles *and* like waves, so there is movement
- The movement of these particles is inherently random, better put: chaotic
- It is *physically impossible* to know both the position and the momentum of a particle at the same time. The more precisely one is known, the less precise the measurement of the other is. It throws science that looks for concrete experiences and findings

- The atomic world is *nothing* like the world we live in, it opens up a whole new way of thinking and viewing the world
- The particles are charged electro magnetically, and will never lose their charge. They are also affecting each other regardless of distance and time.

From a quantum physics perspective, a butterfly that flaps its wings in Brazil, affects the weather in Sri Lanka. This explains how twins, both 'built' with particles that are charged similarly, can perform exactly the same actions, without knowing it from each other, or feeling the same sensations (pain or sadness). Quantum physics also embraces the idea that there is no new energy. All particles have been there forever, they are only re-arranged differently. So, every breathe we take, brings us in contact with energy that has been part of a dinosaur, Albert Einstein or a tree….. to name a few possibilities.

What does this imply for meditation practice?
If everything is built with energy particles, then we as human beings, are just energy. Nothing more, nothing less. And energy affects energy.

Body

Our physical body is built up with firm and dense
energy. We can see our own bodies, other people's
bodies; we can feel them, touch them, we feed our
bodies with firm and dense energy and we make sure
we keep that density going.

Mind

Our mind represents a different alignment of energy
particles. We can't see and touch the mind, but we
know it is there. It centres in our head and has
tentacles going through the dense energy of the body,
as the mind communicates with muscles and organs to
make sure that they act and behave as we want them
to. The mind directs our movements, but the mind also
responds to our emotions. Think of something stressful
and feel your stomach churn. Think of a nerve racking
scenario and your palms will sweat. There is a
connection between the dense energy of the body and
the more subtle energy of the mind, creeping through
the body. The mind is fed by intellectual energy, such
as information in books, or from television, training
such as puzzles and study, etc.

Emotions

A third layer of energy in our beings is emotional or soul energy. More subtle than mental energy, with its core located in the upper-body, stomach area. The emotional energy needs to find its way in the field of the body and mind energy. As it is the subtlest energy of these three. It is also the energy that is most likely to not get the space it needs. Lots of people give priority to the mind or practicalities over emotions. Think of how often you park emotions in favour of 'doing' something else…. Emotional energy can easily be crushed.

In order to feel and be balanced, we need to ensure that we create the space for our three energy 'bodies', so they can flow without obstructions and interact in a natural manner.
All energy bodies are connected and affect each other. Aligning the energy frequencies will help to create a healthy flow, contributing to a healthy human being. If we are healthy we will have no blockages in our energy. The body can function naturally, the mind is doing its job without too much of an effort and we are in touch with our emotions, and allow them to be there.

The battle of the forces

Most of the time we don't have the perfect balance between body, mind and emotions. We sport intensively, focus on our physical body and make that the centre of our being. Too much presence for the body……….. When we stress or worry, we fret endlessly, thinking through different options, implications, causes, errors, and more. Too much presence for the mind…….. When we are overwhelmed with emotions, we can go into total melt-down, forget to look after our body and can't think straight. Too much presence for the emotions…….
In a way, each energy force wants to be top-dog, with the mind as the actual champion.

When we meditate we start a process, lovingly, to soften the energy of all three forces. And when energy is soft, it can flow. When energy is firm and ready for a fight, it bounces, it defends its corners and will not let go.

The meditation starts with calming the mind by forcing it to focus on something, like breathing. The mind then knows that it has a space, it doesn't have to fight for its position and it can just do what you want it to do: focus. This is a great starting point to relax the body and a body scan is a great exercise to soften the energy of the body. It is a type of practice where you address different parts of the body, letting go of tension and tightness. It gives the meditator a deep awareness of the body and is very grounding.

When the mind and body energy is soft and relaxed, you have created space for emotional energy, to just present itself. Which it will do, in whatever form. Sometimes just in colours, sometimes in an awareness of an emotion, sometimes not even noticeable.

What happens during a meditation is that you rest your three energy 'bodies'; you let go of all the unhelpful energies, that you have picked up during a busy day and allow the energy to find its natural flow; a natural flow that is healing.

Sleep gives you a break from awareness, but is not necessarily relaxing the body and the mind or creating space for emotions. Meditation is an activity that aims to relax body, mind and emotions and bring them together in a harmonious flow.

Powerful and magical stuff!

Chapter 3. Misconceptions

There are lots of fantasies surrounding the topic and practice of meditation.
Let me present some of them and dismantle the myth.

Misconception 1 Meditation requires a lot of training to get it right.

As I have mentioned before, meditation is a natural activity, we have all done it, even though we don't consciously remember it. Meditation can be easily re-learned and practiced. It will take only a minute, you can do it anytime, everywhere and it is about doing it. Meditation is only difficult if you become too concerned with doing it right. There is, in fact, no such thing as 'right' or 'wrong' meditation. There is only doing it or not doing it.

Misconception 2 To meditate, you have to turn off your thoughts and make your mind blank.

As you will know by now, your mind is a powerful force and it can't be eliminated. No need for that, anyway. What is needed is that you accept that thoughts will never disappear, or maybe sometimes for a few moments, but they are there, because they have to be. Allowing your thoughts, being gently with them and at the same time, having the discipline to return your focus to your practice is all that needs to be done.

Misconception 3 You have to be good at focussing your attention.

Focussing becomes easier with practice. But it is not about being good, it is about doing. Trying to keep focussed is a very good focusing exercise in itself.

Misconception 4 Meditation is relaxation

Meditation is work, hard work in a relaxed manner, or as I like to mention; it is a 'relaxed effort'. If you let your attention slip, thoughts are coming in and you are losing the focus. Then you work to let go of the thoughts and bring the focus back in. If you fall asleep during your practice, it can only be because you are in a position that allows you to fall asleep, like lying down, so choose a sitting position. If you fall asleep then, your neck and head falling is uncomfortable, and that will wake you up. During a meditation you are in a highly alert state, while relaxing, being very aware and taking control, while letting it flow...... It is like a dance of controversies.

Misconception 5 Meditation is the way to get enlightenment and that is the purpose of the practice.

Pfffff, I don't think so. It might be something that monks in the Himalaya are aiming for, but if you have a job to hold down, a family to organize and a life to live, it is a bit too ambitious. Meditation gives you a tool to create an internal balance that no other technique offers, it gives you a ticket to peace, quick and easy, and it empowers you to create your happiness. That's all. But no enlightenment, please.

Chapter 4. Golden rules for the best practice

Meditation's credo is 'go with the flow', and contradictory, here are some rules that make it easier to go with the flow. Those rules are fundamental for a helpful practice.

Non judgment

Meditation is not about doing it right or wrong. It is just about doing and experiencing it. That is what matters. If you try to focus on your breathing and you continuously 'lose it', because your holiday planning seems to pop up all the time, don't think that you are doing it wrong. It just happens. The only thing for you to do is to observe it, and then go back to focusing on the breathing. The moment you start judging yourself and telling yourself off, you invite an aggressive energy and an internal dialogue will start: 'How silly of me, I can't even do something as simple as concentrate on one thing. I am useless', followed by, 'I want to be able to do it, thoughts go away'. Thoughts then firm up, take up position, pick up the energy and are not moving away, but becoming bigger and more intrusive. Do you recognize that?
Let go of the judgment during your practice.

The next step is to let go of the judgment in normal life situations.

That is a real challenge, as you can only survive in the world by making continuous judgments. A judgment of distance and speed, to decide if you can cross the road; a judgment of cooking time, to decide if your meat is ready; a judgment of planning, to create a realistic things-to-do list. But also a judgment of a person, to decide if it is safe to talk to him/her. A judgment of moods, to decide if you are going to mention a difficult subject….. and so on and so on.

You can't let go of judgments, but you can become aware of them, and then decide what to do. Is it a helpful judgment? Take it on board. Is it irrelevant? Let go of it.

Open mindedness

If you do your meditations with an open mind, you are in for surprises. How about a student who said after a 2 hour workshop: 'I am as high as a kite!' However, if this person expects to feel like that every time he meditates, he is in for a disappointment. Not only that, if you start with an expectation, you are not open to what might happen.

What has happened to me during meditations: I have felt my feet getting warmer and warmer, I have noticed my heartbeat all over my body, I have seen colours, people, pictures, I have felt floaty, I have noticed which isolated muscles in my leg were tired, I noticed pain moving around and disappearing, I have felt sadness, lightness, peace.......

I meditate every morning, and I never know what is going to present itself. So, I just do it and let it happen. Sometimes, it feels as if nothing happens, and that is fine as well. Because I know that my meditation practice is catalyzing positive changes on a deep inner level of my being and I know it manifests itself in how I deal with challenges in daily life.

A great example of open mindedness came to me a few years ago, when I was holidaying on a campsite in the Netherlands, next to a natural lake. The water of the lake, in a country with a relatively cool climate, would usually be cold. And before I jumped in, I already shivered, being overtaken by the experiences I had before.

Then I read a book, which mentioned how expectations can colour your experience in the moment, as you lose your open mindedness. The next day I went to the lake, ready to dive in, but with a different mindset. Standing on the side, looking at the beautiful lake, I refused to think about the temperature. I was just going to swim. I dived in and had an extraordinary experience. For the first few seconds, I just felt how soft the water was, how my body got wet, how I moved in it, and then....... Yes, then I felt that it was quite cold. But not being narrowed down by an expectation, made my experience of diving into a lake, much richer and less cold – at least for a few seconds.

Another lesson in open mindedness was taught by my 3 year old son. He had been pestering me for weeks about visiting the loft. As the loft was only accessible via an aluminium loft ladder, I was not keen for him to get there. However, at one point I gave in and let him go up. I was following and holding him, to prevent him falling down.

When he stepped into the loft, I heard a deep sigh and then an amazed 'awesome, oooohhhh, awesome'. He waddled on his chubby legs, pointing at the round window, which was covered in cob webs, with the sunrays shining through and said 'awesome'. He touched the boxes, where all sorts of stuff was sticking out and kept on saying 'awesome'.

He made me realize that I thought about the loft as a heap of rubbish, dirt, useless stuff that needed to go and had nothing going for it. Looking through his eyes, I had a totally different experience, and could see how my loft space was awesome, mysterious, secretive, exciting!

Acceptance

Accept whatever happens during your practice. Don't fight it, just accept. This is about experiences you might judge as positive or negative. But as you try not to judge, you accept whatever appears: warmth, discomfort, pain, thoughts, colours, peaceful feelings, anything.

It might be difficult to accept that you are feeling pain, but if you are busy fighting with your pain, how can you experience just going with the flow, or being in the moment or feeling inner peace?

When you are practicing, it is not easy to accept that thoughts are
popping in and seem to spoil it. But it doesn't matter. Thoughts are a natural product of the mind, and it is one of the ways that stored up stress is released in meditation.

As you continue meditating, you will discover that you can experience deep relaxation and inner peace, even when there are thoughts in your mind.

Acceptance in daily life makes life in itself a lot easier. There are always situations that are out of your control, and regardless of whether you agree or disagree, that won't change. The only thing that changes is your mood, as non-acceptance is frustrating and unhelpful. Acceptance doesn't mean you agree, but it colours your internal response and offers a starting point to create changes.

The serenity prayer reflects that in its core:

God, grant me the serenity to accept the things I cannot change,
The courage to change the things I can,
And the wisdom to know the difference.

These three rules: non-judgment, open mindedness and acceptance should be part of your meditation practice, but their real value will present itself when you start noticing you apply the rules in your daily life. It will certainly make your life less stressed.

Chapter 5. What do cats have to do with it?

Cats, the added value in mindfulness

Can you picture this: connecting with the silence within, feeling peaceful and calm, sitting in stillness...... My hectic life comes to a standstill, while I retreat into a meditation. I focus my mind (which can be quite hard work) and relax at the same time. I feel good and it is lovely to know that there is someone in my life, who is always on the lookout to share that feeling with me: my 14 year old fluffy cat Norton!

As soon as I am 5 minutes into my meditation, I will feel his warm and soft body draped against my leg, my bum or even on top of me. Combined with content purring we continue our mutual visit of peaceful places.

What does this tell us? As I change the busy energy that is usually around me (being physically and mentally active) for the calm energy that comes with the meditation, I attract beings that live more intuitively than humans.

A survey about cats and cat owners put forward the question: 'Do cats meditate?' One of the answers was: 'Cats are very zen creatures, very good at the art of simply being. I would bet that they get to that meditative state of mind without all the breathing and mantra stuff that we humans have to do to get there.'

I guess, I agree with this statement, as far as meditation relates to the art of 'simply being' and 'acceptance'.
I don't agree with the statement, if I describe meditation as a relaxed effort. When we meditate we are definitely busy! Busy with keeping our mind focussed on an object or activity of choice. And when the mind wanders off, we bring it back to the original focus. Time and time again. That way we prevent ourselves from falling asleep and activate ourselves getting into 'the zone', a state of awareness where we can rest and just 'be', because the mind doesn't distract us. When in 'the zone' we allow other experiences to be and with a heightened awareness we notice a lot about our bodies and our emotions and often can have light bulb moments.

If you sit still sometimes, and your cat comes to you, attracted by your calmer energy, you can change your chilling out session into a meditation, if you close your eyes and focus the whole of your awareness on an aspect of your cat's presence; this can be his breathing/purring, the warmth of his body or just how he smells.

Just try to do this for 10 minutes: work on keeping focussed on what you decide to focus on, and observe how good and rested you feel afterwards.

I doubt that your cat (or mine) is doing the same practice: working hard at focussing and keeping the mind occupied, so he will get into 'the zone'.

I suspect my Norton is just happily snoring, loving calm company and totally unaware......

Chapter 6. Letting go of pain.........

What is pain? Pain is an indication that something is not right……. It is a valuable warning system that helps us to take action and help ourselves to stay healthy.

Pain is also a concentration of energy, blocking the natural flow in our system and this block can be very uncomfortable.
Sometimes we are stuck with the pain, we have to go through it as it is part of a process towards healing.

However, you can learn to experience pain in a less intrusive manner. When I do my talk 'An introduction to meditation', I invite non-experienced meditators to get in touch with pain. And we then do a practice of observing and disengaging. This helps to relieve the sensations of pain.
Very powerful and very helpful!

I went through an eye test with no discomfort. Can you believe it? It sounds too good to be true.
But it is!

I was subjected to a nasty eye test, with lots of drops, poking and bright light. Sitting with my chin on a stand, forehead gripped in a band and 'Just look straight forward please' was the setting. Not easy to stay still,

not easy not to produce a flood of tears and sneezing and squeezing. And of course, I felt tense. Being under attack with eyes wide open is a tense situation.
And then, all of a sudden it dawned on me that this was a situation where I could apply my dis-engagement skills, something I do regularly in normal life and the skill I train during a meditation.

What I mean is that I step out of the physical sensations and step into a mindful state. I don't engage with what goes on, but I do observe what goes on. It is as if I am an outsider.
The beauty of this process is that it allows me to distance myself from the physical sensations and therefore, I don't feel the pain!

Research shows that the brain activity in the primary somatosensory cortex, an area that is crucially involved in creating the feeling of pain (where in the body and the intensity), is significantly lower during and after meditation. At the same time the brain is boosting the coping mechanism. In one of the studies the meditators exposed to strong pain stimuli experienced a pain level close to zero.

In another study, researchers mildly burned 15 men and women in a lab on two separate occasions, before and after the volunteers attended four 20-minute meditation training sessions over the course of four days. During the second go-round, when the participants were instructed to meditate, they rated the exact same pain stimulus -- a 120-degree heat on their calves -- as being 57 per cent less unpleasant and 40 per cent less intense, on average.

If you are suffering from pain, you know how draining and distracting it is. Popping pills can give some relief, but is never a healthy solution. What is healthy and natural, is using meditation to reduce your pain.

Jon Kabat-Zinn is a pioneer of using mindfulness for pain. This is what he says about pain. 'Physical pain is the response of the body and the nervous system to a huge range of stimuli that are perceived as noxious, damaging, or dangerous. There are really three dimensions to pain: the physical or sensory component; the emotional or affective component, how we feel about the sensation; and the cognitive component, the meaning we attribute to our pain. Take the situation that you have got a pain in your back. You can't lift your children; getting in and out of the car is difficult; you can't even sit in meditation. Maybe you can't even work. That is the physical component. But as you have to give up a lot, you will have feelings about that—anger, probably—and in due course, you are susceptible to depression. That is the emotional response. And then you have thoughts about the pain—questions about what caused it,

negative stories about what is going to happen. Those expectations, projections, and fears compound the stress of the pain, eroding the quality of your life.
There is a way to work with all this, based on Buddhist meditative practices, which can liberate you, to a very large extent, from the experience of pain. Whether or not you can reduce the level of sensory pain, the affective and cognitive contributions to the pain— which make it much worse—(usually) can be lessened. And then, very often, the sensory component of the pain changes as well.
The key point is to change your relationship to the pain by opening up to it and paying attention to it. You sort of welcome the pain. Not because you're masochistic, but because the pain is there. So you need to understand the nature of the experience and the possibilities for, as the doctors might put it, learning to live with it," or, as the Buddhists might put it, "liberation from the suffering." If you distinguish between pain and suffering, change is possible. As the saying goes, "Pain is inevitable; suffering is optional." - Jon Kabat-Zinn in an interview a few years ago.

There have been studies looking at how the mind processes acute pain at the sensory level. Subjects are randomized between two groups, and given the cold presser test, where a tourniquet is placed around the bicep, followed by putting the arm into ice water.

There's no more blood flow, so the arm gets very painful very fast. They measure how long someone can keep the arm in the water, related to an attentional strategy or a mindfulness strategy. This strategy involves paying attention to the sensations, really moving into them and being with them as nonjudgmentally as you can. Another measure is how long someone can keep the arm in the water, related to a distraction strategy, which involves thinking about other things and in doing so, tuning out of the pain. What the study showed was that in the early minutes of having the arm in the ice water, distraction works better than mindfulness. People were less aware of the discomfort because they were telling themselves a story, or remembering something, or having a fantasy. But after the arm is in the cold water for a while, mindfulness becomes much more powerful than distraction, when it comes to tolerating the pain. This indicates that mindfulness can offer support to chronic pain sufferers.

My first deliberate application of meditation for pain relief was during labour. I did very well, coped easily with mild contractions, but….. That all changed when I was given medication to speed up the process (called induction). My body did what it had to do, but instead of taking 4 hours, it took 20 minutes. It is like missing the warming-up! The shock for my system was so severe that I could only be in the pain; engulfed in it and there was no way that I could concentrate on the techniques I had applied earlier. So, when the going gets tough, it can be very difficult. I wonder how I would do now, after more than a decade of daily practice, but it is a bit too much to get pregnant to find out.

It will remain a mystery......

7. How schools can perform better

Research shows that a mindfulness meditation changes the brain, and helps someone to perform better in cognitive tasks.

How does that happen?

- There is less rumination , which helps a better focus
- Boosts the working memory, the active part of your memory system, which enables us to process information and at the same time work with it: our mental multi -tasking unit
- The emotional reactivity decreases, leading to less emotional distraction and equally less stress

Several studies have been done into the effect of meditation on the performance during an exam. One study facilitated a group of students to meditate, just before an exam. The exam takers did not meditate by themselves. The results were clear: meditating before an exam results in a higher score. Of course, if you can focus better, have your working memory in full swing and are not plagued by stress reactions, there are no distractions and you can put all your energy into the test itself.

Other studies showed similar outcomes.

Curriculum

Another survey showed that 70% of teenagers suffer from stress. The main causes being the pressure around study. Homework, tests and exams were pointed out as the biggest source of stress for 55%, where 15% of the students mentioned the emotional aspects of achieving and not-achieving as the main cause of stress.

For teenagers the immediate effects of stress are loss of sleep, concentration problems, mood swings, self-esteem issues, low energy levels, headaches, digestive problems amongst others. Immediate consequences are lower grades and academic underachievement. In the long term stress is causing depression. Both undesirable situations.

Victims of the system?

If we want children to be educated, we ideally want them to enjoy the process, so they can continue during their life to study and grow their knowledge base and improve their chances of great and fulfilling careers, without turning into nervous wrecks.

The focus on following a solid curriculum does not allow for extra-curricular activities, which teaches youngsters life skills that are actually crucial if they want to perform and achieve in the regular curriculum. The narrow mindedness within the current school systems in lots of countries, is not helping the next generation. I would like my children to be all-rounders, having developed a range of skills that incorporate academic knowledge, but certainly social skill and life skill on how to manage themselves and keep themselves safe and sound.

As a result of stress they are not able to study properly: "When I start my homework I can only think of the upcoming test and it makes my stomach cramp. I then can only think of my stomach, so in the end I don't learn anything", as 14 year old Tina told me. Another student Anthony, aged 20, had big issues with exams. "I prepare myself well. I even enjoy the studying, but when it comes to performing at an exam I always underachieve. When I start reading the questions, it is as if my knowledge disappears and I can't think anymore. I just go totally blank. And it gets worse and worse."

What can we do?
Teaching this generation to meditate in demanding exam situations, will give them a skill for life. If we could only incorporate meditation in what schools offer, the world of study would be a better place. And if private schools, keen on academic results, step out of their comfort zone and introduce meditation into the curriculum, they would do better. If only they realised......

My experience

I recently did a programme with teenagers in a school. The budget was limited, so we could only teach 3 sessions (lasting 50 minutes). It was an absolutely brilliant experience for me. To see those kids coming in the class room: girls all chatty and very busy, boys sort of slumming, hanging in their chairs, working very hard to look not interested........ but I could sense their curiosity.

The first session we talked about stress, how it affects your thoughts, feelings and behaviour and then we did some very basic meditation practices. Short, simple and effective. It was great to notice the surprise in most of the teens, when they were asked to tell us what happened and how they felt.
A new world had opened.
Most of these teenagers felt very tense around their upcoming exams and we asked them to do a little meditation before they started their homework. A practice that would take no more than 3 minutes. However, one boy shook his head and said that his mum would never agree with him wasting time like that...... Such a shame, to be closed off to the world of new experiences.

The students got about 10 different practices they could do, before homework, before a test and even during a test, to give themselves a refreshing break.

The feedback was fantastic. The ones who took on board the new learning all reported back that they felt so much better and calmer, during the preparation and the exam itself. They were also all happy with the results.

I am not claiming that the results are better than they would be without the practice, as there is no real proof for that. But a personal perception of feeling calmer is a great achievement and reason enough to promote simple meditation amongst students and exam candidates. Regardless of age!

Chapter 8. Sharing your shower

One of the few moments in our busy lives that we can be just by ourselves, with no disturbances, is when we are in the shower. Well, is it?

Are you fully aware of what is going on when you step under the hot water, reach for the shampoo and start massaging your limbs?

Most of us take a shower in the morning. Let's go through the motions: the alarm goes, you wake up, struggle away from the duvet and move towards the bathroom. You perform a range of habitual and necessary actions before you set foot in the cubicle to feel the dancing hot water drops on your head, shoulders and arms.

Mmmmmm, nice wake-up.

You take a deep breath, think about the day ahead and all of a sudden your shower cubicle is filled with your colleagues, your family members, your things-to-do list…… WOW, and they all fit in that cubicle!!!!!

What are you doing to yourself? You stepped out of your own life, that very moment that you invited these other persons and things into your cubicle.

Mindfulness guru Jon Kabat-Zinn is one of the main people in the mindfulness movement. A gentle person, with a clear vision of the benefits of mindfulness meditation and being in the now. He mentioned the shower example and what he meant to demonstrate is that there are many moments in our life when we are not fully alive, because we are not connected to ourselves. We invite 'strangers' in, we leave the current pleasure of BEING and we live the non-reality of the future, which takes place out of the current time, place, and space.

If you don't feel connected, if you feel lost, overwhelmed or out of control, the easiest way to get to a better place is to get connected with yourself by doing a mindfulness practice.

Mindfulness and meditation are terms that are sometimes used to point out the same thing. Mindfulness definitions can focus on:

- Action - Jon Kabat-Zinn, defines mindfulness as, "paying attention in a particular way: on purpose, in the present moment, and non-judgementally. In my opinion this is the definition of a type of meditation, to get into a state of mindfulness.

- State - David Black, a US therapist, says:
  "mindfulness is now widely considered to be an
  inherent quality of human consciousness. That
  is, a capacity of attention and awareness
  oriented to the present moment that varies in
  degree within and between individuals, and can
  be assessed empirically and independent of
  religious, spiritual or cultural beliefs."
- Opposite (no clear source): mindfulness is the
  process of waking up from a life lived on
  automatic pilot and based in habitual
  responding.

I embrace the definition for meditation = all activities
that support the state of being mindful. Being mindful
means existing in the moment, being fully aware, and
feeling closely connected to oneself.

The benefits

Research has shown that mindfulness meditation
affects 4 different aspects of human life significantly.

Regulates emotions

Mindfulness mediation practice promotes cognitive
awareness and decreases rumination, because the
brain disengages from cognitive activities (active

thinking), and enhances attentional capacities. The brain enhances the working memory; and these help to develop effective strategies to regulate emotion. Not only during the practice, but also afterwards.

In one study, a group of mindfulness meditators was exposed to a sad film, before they started their 8 week meditation course and after they had done the course.

The results were self-reporting lower scores around feelings of depression and anxiety. Measures with an MRI scan showed a different neural activity; much lower in the part of the brain that causes stress and anxiety (amygdala).

This indicates that mindfulness changes the working of the brain, helps us to become selective of emotions and able to choose positive ones instead of negative ones.

Reduction of anxiety, depression and distress

Clinical studies have shown that depression and other mental health issues change and make patients feel happier. This is also seen in changes of the physical brain. Scans, photography and electromagnetic measurements show a decrease in size of certain parts of the brain and an increase in others. If you envisage the brain as a muscle and meditation as a training, it makes perfect sense.

An important part of our brain, the prefrontal cortex has a right and left side, which operate differently but together always make up 100%. This means that as one bit declines, the other bit grows.
The left side is related to a way of looking at life events with acceptance, curiosity, love and kindness ('Approach or Embrace').
The right side is related to fear, disgust, aversion and denial ('Avoidance'). Meditation increases the left side of the brain, supporting us to face the challenges of life with a mind set that is open, inquisitive and positive. The right side however, supports anger, aggression, stress and negativity.

Better achievements

Studies show the effects of meditation on the results in tests; students, who practiced mindfulness before entering an exam situation, scored significantly higher than the group who did not practice. These studies evolved around several test situations.

Improvement in physical health

Stress has an impact on the body and meditators have shown reduction in blood pressure, reduction of heart conditions, less digestive issues, less migraines, etc.

When NOT to be mindful.....

Mindfulness is helpful in most situations. However, I choose NOT to be mindful when I don't want to engage. And that is particularly true, when I talk to my mother on the phone. We are not very in tune with each other and I decided a long time ago that it doesn't make sense for us to have an engaging conversation. We communicate on completely different wave lengths and don't seem to be able to find each other. It have discovered that if I am conversing with her on automatic pilot, she feels good about our talk and I do too, as I just hang in there.

Another situation when I don't engage is when I do my domestic chores. Feeling resentful, unfulfilled and that I am wasting my time, it makes it easier for me to do it in a mindless manner.

Preferably, while talking to my mother…..

Chapter 9. Murdered peacefully...............

One sunny morning, when I got up at my usual 6am to go downstairs for my meditation, I decided to sit and practice in the conservatory, as the sun was lighting that area with the promise of a beautiful Spring day. I was joined by my cat Norton, who always seems to like our sessions, almost more than I do.

Meditation is the very simple action of removing yourself from anything else but... and zooming into the focus of the practice. This can be the breathing, the body, chakras, or other things. That morning I decided to focus my meditation on the body.

When I focus and try to zoom in, the experience of what I am focussing on becomes more intense. I notice sensations and vibrations of something that is always there, but when I don't concentrate on it, I don't notice. It is a bit similar to the woman who wants to get pregnant and all of a sudden sees pregnant ladies on every occasion and in every situation.

So, here I am. Concentrating on my body, the sensations, the vibrations, the tension, the relaxation...... and all the time, working to stay disengaged from what I observe.

Sitting in the sun, feeling the warmth of the sun on my face. Not judging, not engaging, just being with it. Then, observing a sensation in my hair. At the back of my head I could definitely feel some hairs moving, going from the left to the right. And then a hair moving on my cheek and hairs on my forehead! It is an interesting sensation, and I have to admit that it was a real challenge to not engage with that tickly feeling. I stuck with it for what seemed a long time.

Feeling tickling sensations, just observing, keeping the detachment…………………………….. And then…………… it became too much.

I felt sensations and tickling on my forehead, which was different from before, more intense and getting to the point of being unbearable. I decided to get up and check out what was going on. It couldn't keep the zen going….

Walking to the kitchen, followed by the cat, I picked up a hand mirror and kept it to my face. Leaning towards the window, over the sink, I saw what caused my challenge. A small, but no doubt perfectly formed little insect was walking over my forehead. I had a good look, no panic involved, still a bit affected by my meditative state!

And I decided to shake him (or her) off, the little bugger. I dumped him, in the sink. I knew he couldn't survive, I knew I was responsible for ending his life, but I chose to do it anyway. He had to go.

Feeling ambivalent I returned to the sofa to continue my meditation. Feeling sorry for the little nit, who just enjoyed our meditation, hopefully as much as I did….

As a consolation, I know he went in peace…….

Chapter 10. Ditch the diets

Weight loss is a topic that never leaves the lime light, which indicates that there is no solution for this recurring challenge. A recent study mentioned that only 20% of ex-dieters were able to keep the weight off. People with a tendency to have uncontrolled eating sessions and those who suffered depression were amongst the 80% who regained their weight.

These figures show that weight loss is heavy duty, and not as simple as just taking in less calories, doing a bit more exercise and showing some will power.

I know the biggest part of the weight loss has to do with the emotional aspects . As an EX bulimic for over 20 years (and having totally left that behind), I know the biggest challenge is that we enter into a BATTLE. We enter the battle with our fat reserves, we dislike or even hate those, and we gear ourselves up for a war. A war we are going to win, at least that is what we tell ourselves.
From the perspective of stress and stress management, the following happens: whenever we are attacked, we fight back. Sometimes this is an obvious, external action, sometimes this is an internal and mostly subconscious process.

When it comes to weight loss, we can distinguish two internal 'personalities', who are engaging in an internal dialogue. One is the person who talks to the outside world, the attacker, the other one is the person inside who has a different agenda, the defender.

Take a step back and consider……

What happens when someone points an accusing finger towards you? Physically you are tensing up, your brain starts producing and releasing adrenaline and cortisol, the famous stress hormones, and the whole of your being goes massively into defence, not wanting to give in. Your automatic response to attack is defence.

The battle about weight has a clear attacker, the head, and a sneaky defender, the heart. The head is telling us, as will our partner, friends or our dreams, to lose weight. The heart gives us another message: it is nice to be able to hide behind our extra pounds, or I am still rebelling against my parents and this is my power tool, or I do not want to live up to expectations….. and more and more.
This internal battlefield will prevent you being successful with your weight loss.

Meditation helps in becoming accepting and non-judgmental of your current situation. The part of your brain that is curious, willing to embrace a challenge and more positive (the left pre frontal cortex) is more active, than the part of your brain (the right pre frontal cortex) that is aggressive and negative.

A relaxed attitude and a deeply seated positive approach to making changes, will support every dieter on a successful journey.

Chapter 11. How to do it

'Tranquility can be reached by taking no action.'

Meditation is a skill we can all easily learn again. When we are young, we live so intuitively that we know when it is time to retreat into our own silent space. Look at babies, when they are content in their cot, eyes open and fully concentrating on one little something: a shadow on the wall, a moving mobile, a sound. And they are totally involved with their whole being in the experience. In doing this their mind is calming down, and they reach a meditative state. When life evolves we seem to lose that natural ability. Life around us is so busy, always offering something that distracts us from our inner stillness. If we deprive ourselves and our mind of a regular rest, we get stressed. When we get too much stress, we get ill and become unhappy.

Meditation is easy.

Deep down inside us we all have the experience, we all have the intuitive knowledge. Unfortunately, the busy-ness of our lives prevents us from being in touch with intuition, so instead of doing or being, we start thinking about it. What is it? How does it work? Will I do it right? What model shall I use for meditation?

Meditation is about focusing.

But what to focus on?

One of the fun challenges is to find out what works for you. As everybody is unique, everyone has their preferences, which might change over time.

The main types of focus are:

Body scanning
You have probably done a guided body scan, where you 'visit' different parts of your body and either just observe those, or try to bring in relaxation. It is usually very effective.

Movement
Using your body in movement is an excellent way of focussing, e.g. meditating. When you move your body, you usually have to concentrate, otherwise you stumble. There is a slow walking meditation that starts off very wobbly, but when it progresses in time, the focus gets stronger and the walking gets steadier. It is a great way to get rid of stress.

Breathing
Traditionally, breathing has played an important role in meditation.

Senses

When focussing on one particular sense, you will get a really intensive experience. Try it with your hearing. Close your eyes and just listen. Listen to the sounds around you. The longer you do that for, the more you will hear.

Another lovely focus can be a candle. Look at a candle light and just notice what happens……….. Great fun!

Energy focus (chakras, energy flow)

Once you have mastered softening your energy, you will be able to notice different energies and centres in your body. Chakras are 'wheels of energy' that help to heal both body and mind. There are different meditations you can do, focussing on chakras.

Spiritual focus (love, peace, light)

Meditate by breathing in love, or light is a practice that can lead to interesting new sensations and feelings. The after affect will be strong and it will help you to stay calm when the busy-ness takes off

Loving kindness (to develop compassion towards self and others)

This is a more spiritual approach, and will work well for some, not so good for others.

My suggestion is to experiment with different focuses to discover what you like and what works for you.

More about the body scan

The practice of the body scan is a way of relaxing the body. By focussing on different parts of the body and trying to let go of tension, it is easy to get into a state of deep relaxation. It is also an easy way to experience the feeling of being in a meditative state and to be able to switch off. Especially for those who think they can't switch off, it works very well. The benefits your get from doing a body scan practice are (at least) threefold:

1. **Resting the body**

A deep bodily relaxation allows the physical body to rest and recuperate. As meditation not only helps recovery through lowering cortisol levels and reducing the inflammation response, the deliberate relaxation of the muscles helps them to get a deep rest. Many professional athletes incorporate meditation into their training to achieve faster rebounds from intense workouts.

2. **Relaxing the mind**

A guided body scan will help the mind to focus. You don't have to actively engage your mind to practice as all instructions will be given. Listening to those stops the mind from wandering and as a result the mind will rest.

3. Energising your whole being

Resting both body and mind for long enough, will give an even greater benefit: energy. The deliberate relaxation opens us up to receive more energy and more focussed. If you are a 'mid-afternoon-napper', because you need to top up your energy, try a body scan instead of a sleep. During sleep you are not necessarily relaxing the body (we clinch our fists, and grind our teeth even when we sleep!) or the mind (still thinking about your things to do list or solving the world's problems), so your rest is limited. But, practicing the body scan will give you an extra deep rest.

Mariette's body scan is available as a download: http://stressfreecoaching.co.uk/buy-now/

More about breathing

Breathing is the process that moves air in and out of the lungs. Humans need oxygen to release energy via respiration, in the form of the metabolism of energy-rich molecules such as glucose. Breathing is only one process that delivers oxygen to where it is needed in the body and removes carbon dioxide. Another important process involves the movement of blood by the circulatory system. Gas exchange occurs in the pulmonary alveoli by passive diffusion of gases between the alveolar gas and the blood in lung capillaries. Once these dissolved gases are in the blood, the heart powers their flow around the body (via the circulatory system).

In addition to removing carbon dioxide, breathing results in loss of water from the body. Exhaled air has a relative humidity of 100% because of water diffusing across the moist surface of breathing passages and alveoli.

There is more to breathing........

Breathing is both a sub-conscious process (i.e., your body keeps breathing automatically whether you think about breathing or not), and a conscious process (i.e., you can take it out of "automatic" mode, and consciously control it - breathe fast, slow, deeply, shallow, hold your breath, etc.).

Thus, breathing is a bridge between the sub-conscious and conscious minds. It is a vehicle to integrate aspects of our being. It feeds the physical body, calms emotions, helps to focus the mind and it is also our link to etheric, philosophical or spiritual areas. We are given life, and given breath. For those who believe in some kind of "plan", flow or God involved in the universe, you could say that it breathes each breathe into us. When we cease breathing, our body ceases to live.

Breath links us to everyone else. Think of all the billions of molecules in each breath of air we breathe in and out. How many have been breathed by others? Throughout history, and in the present, there is a chance that one of those molecules was breathed by...

In many of the meditation techniques you'll find, the breath is a common denominator. And there are many ways on offer about how to use it and approach it.

Some examples:
- Control your breathing
- Meditate on your breathing
- Leave it to the subconscious mind
- Watch your body breathe
- Concentrate on the process of breathing
- Integrate your breathing with relaxing
- Use your breathing to let go

What is the function of breathing?
- Fuelling the body cells with oxygen. No breath, no oxygen, no life!
- Cleansing the body and the cells. By exchanging the gaseous waste for fresh air.

- Purifying. Deep breathing to overflow the cells and add more goodness.
- De-stressing / regulating emotions. Emotions flow on the breath; is it the emotion that rules the breath or the breath that rules the emotion?
- Energising. Making the body, mind and emotions feeling more alive.

Obstacles for effective breathing

What gets in the way of relaxed and easy breathing is: a blocked nose or a cold; tightness in the chest; tight fitting clothes; a full stomach and a poor posture.
Top Tips to Breathe Better
Breathing consciously will make a huge difference to your general health and well-being.
In order to breathe better, do the following:
- Make the conscious decision to focus on your breathing
- Set a timer, so you are not distracted by timekeeping. Any time between one minute and half an hour …..
- Sit comfortably, with straight back, don't slump
- Make sure you will not be interrupted, so switch off phone
- Do not wear tight clothes
- Relax your shoulders

- Relax your abdomen
- Relax facial muscles
- Fill abdomen with air, then fill lungs, empty abdomen before lungs and pull belly in, then empty lungs; create a wave-like motion
- Make out-breath longer than in-breath, ideally twice as long
- Keep in control of the muscles that are engaging in the breathing process
- Enjoy the breathing practice and the effects

When starting your practice, it will help to find a space that is comfortable. Set aside just 5 to 10 minutes – maybe set a timer -, and keep sensory input under control. If it helps you, put on some music, no lyrics as that will engage your mind and take your control away.

Guidance for your practice

Put some music on, that doesn't evoke memories and doesn't have lyrics as these will distract you from focussing. Sit comfortably with your feet on the floor, close your eyes and breathe in through the nose, out through the nose. Cool air coming in, warm air going out…….

Then choose something to focus on. And just focus on that, for the length of time you have set aside.

To help you get going, you can download for free a 5 minute focussing exercise:

http://stressfreecoaching.co.uk/free-download-book/

I have recorded a CD with guided meditations: 1 minute, 3 minutes, 5 minutes and half an hour, which you can purchase from the website. This is the link: http://stressfreecoaching.co.uk/bullshit-downloads/

Your meditation will help you to reach a state of mindfulness, a way of being in the moment: there is no past, because it is gone; there is no future, because it is a fantasy; there is only the now. And 'the now' offers a powerful, positive energy, because it just is and doesn't allow for judgments, resistance, anger or other negative emotions.

It is not easy to be 'in the now', as we are distracted continuously by our mind.

Things to do lists, planning, thoughts about other people – most likely at this very moment while you are reading this, those three things are going on at the same time. No wonder we can feel depleted of energy, no wonder we get stressed.

I have felt in myself and seen in others the amazing changes once meditation has been taken up as a regular activity. It doesn't need to take a lot of time, and it is not difficult.

That is all.

Easy peasy!

Conclusion

You know more about meditation now, how easy it can be, how much fun it can be and how it can help you to improve your life.

No mysteries, no bullshit, just a lot of common-sense. I hope this encourages you to pick up the practice, because if you feel calmer, more in control and at peace, the world around you will be calmer and at peace. A little drop in the ocean of the world, that helps to make the world a better place.

I would love to help you with it. For a start get the download, that is mentioned on page 75 for free. If you like it, you might want to buy the CD. And of course, get in touch to discuss what might be a good way forward for you.

I am organising talks, workshops, courses and also offer individual tuition. As the work is developing, more will be coming.

To keep informed and to receive my tips, you can email me at mariette@stressfreecoaching.co.uk and write
FREE SUBSCRIPTION REQUEST in the title.
I will then put you on my mailing list.

Stay in touch, stay tuned and keep mindful.

Go well,

Mariette

Lightning Source UK Ltd.
Milton Keynes UK
UKOW05f0807230414

230441UK00008B/50/P